MOODS IN BLOOM

An anthology of poems
with illustrative photographs

Copyright © 2021 Meryl M Williams

All rights reserved, including the right to reproduce this book, or portions thereof in any form. No part of this text may be reproduced, transmitted, downloaded, decompiled, reverse engineered, or stored, in any form or introduced into any information storage and retrieval system, in any form or by any means, whether electronic or mechanical without the express written permission of the author.

ISBN: 978-1-915889-30-0

MOODS IN BLOOM

An anthology of poems
with illustrative photographs

By
Meryl M Williams

THE POET MERYL M WILLIAMS
b1966

Meryl was born in South Wales and studied biological sciences in Cardiff, London, Bath and Texas USA before returning to Bath and writing poetry and prose.

She has previously published a selection of books of poetry titled "Mementoes in Verse", "Reflections of Time", "Doodles, Dog Ears and Ditties" and "A Boy's Anthem". Other works by Meryl are a short story compilation called "Andrew's Amazing Odyssey and Other Stories", and two novelettes titled "The Judge Jones Trilogy" and "My Lady's Sovereign".

Meryl is inspired by the beauties of Nature but also city scenery, amazing feats of engineering and the wonderful people that have supported her journey, making everything possible.

In this new departure for the poet, photographs are added to illustrate the new verse. The title of this anthology reflects the uplift in mood as spring returns and brightly coloured blooms are once more on display around the parks and gardens.

In this anthology, the poem "I am Regime" had won Highly Commended in the Koestler Trust Awards.

MOODS IN BLOOM

THE MISSING SPIDER

Storm Arwen blew its way
Through hedges, tree tops, more
I went to find a web
But all were gone away

Not a spider to be seen
Hidden 'neath winter greens
So at eventide I sought
The mysterious arachnoid
Busy weaving lace
But no, not a trace

Then the beast returned
Clinging perilously from walls
So where has it been
While non evident and unseen?

Who knows the spider's tale?
But its resurgence is renowned
For there it is again
While winds they blow, as rain beats down.

LAMBS TAILS

Colder, darker, lagging dawn
But here's a sign of spring
Pale against these barren leaves
Tender, trembling, green catkins

Rain or frost does not deter
They hold as winds howl round
Speaking of a bright New Year
A welcome sight without a sound
Like lambs tails growing over ground
A sweet, miraculous thing

I left them to enjoy the wild
As weather warms at last
Forbearing to pluck these early blooms
That don't survive my heated rooms
Or live without the frost

Here's to Nature, dance or sing
My toast to every living thing
For when I grow too old to care
Then mine is not a worthy heart.

MY YELLOW PHASE

Sunshine, yellow roses
Impatiens, pansies, fruit
All things yellow just
Fill me with delight
When days are dark and cold
Both outside or within
A touch of cheer lights up my life
For many colours soothe, inspire, excite
The darkest night, so cold alone
Can be a harbinger of a golden dawn
Hues, tones of honey uplift like never before
For as I feel such deep remorse
I lament a darker shore.
My yellow phase will come and go
But many things don't change
The power of sunshine or healing rain
The love of friends, my inner gains
Relieve me from all woe.

FEELING CIRCULAR

A window on the world
Reflects my inner strengths
I've seen a hidden light
Soft glow refresh the fight
For battles weary onward go
So many were left behind
Their faces come before me now
All names, all loved by rights
Do you remember Freddy?
For what became of Jo?
And who is Janet, Mike or Jane?
You seem to know them all.
But there's one thing for certain
You're here and so am I
So let's enjoy the good times
We're all too young to die
Before you go think of me
Locked in a hidden prayer
Softly walk towards me
Then join me everywhere
As circles within circles
Return from start to end
I'll end at your beginning
For you'll always be my friend.

LOOKING UP

Bright, blazing, beautiful blue sky
Thinking how good, how healing
Darker, sombre colours washed away
Light ends a storm of weeping
Gazing upwards through the leaves
Dappled yellows, browns and green
A shadow here, a squirrel there
The winter life abounds.
Sorrow gone, a surge of joy
A gift I wrapped for you
I hope it brings you life and peace
A lull from strife, a rest from pain
A morning lift, the end of year
Fresh starts we hope, we cheer.

HARVEST MOON

As dusk descends with gathering gloom
A host of pied wagtails flock to town
I don't remember any sound
Just a dozen wagtails all around
The pale, silver glow of a full, full moon
Rises gently then birds have flown
Black and White with feathers flicking
Their evening meet is God's own greeting

Each winter day they come the same
But more this once than ever seen
To count each one as more arrive
A challenge as they quickly leave
Above an earthly flicker of unrest
The harvest moon appears as blessed
Bright to lighten hurrying beasts
Until the Dawn and timely rest.

MORNING MISTS

Drizzle damping silent falls
Mist lingers over vales and hills
Morning mood of bright hope lasts
Until the rain persistent soaks
Into a sodden earth, plunged beneath
Its winter wet.

But now the shortest day is done
Longer times will see the sun
For as mist rolls over land and sea
Heaven declares a time of peace
A child has come to lead the way
Until a bright more hopeful day.

Shrouded now the hilltop far
Features smothered, fog pea soup thick
My mind relives a generation
To hear the horn along the coast
For danger is at large for all
Who in the Channel cross the seas,
Waiting, waiting for a breeze.

IN SPRINGFIELD PARK

A walk in autumn's golden glow
Sees fallen leaves with branches bare
This spacious landscape touched by frost
Is lovely any time of year

The cherry blossom led to fruit
A walnut tree drinks from the spring
This hazel copse provides a shade
A home for every living thing

Standing on its southern edge
I looked towards my western past
For there beheld a wondrous sight
One new, one old, the Severn Bridge

Clear days are special here
Once fog has melted with the dawn
For I have risen, no alarm I need
I fly to cook, to clean, to feed

We remember on this, a lovely day
That freedom found will always stay.

GROWING OLD GRACEFULLY

I gaze with deepest love
Upon these kindly hands
That hold a pen, or click a mouse
Or rest in folded mode
As we talk of all things prose

But should my thoughts fly from you
They never stray that far
The gentle ties that bind you
Will hold you close and fast

For a muse is esoteric
And we can never share
Those joys of other lovers
Which cause so many tears

So sit for just a short while
Remember me today
Tomorrow never nears us
Our yesterdays are gone
This moment you're my own.

ART FOR ART'S SAKE

Like a glorious, tumbling waterfall
I surround myself with paint
But will the viewer understand
My own unique and personal taste?

I draw to lose my substance
For Art is ethereal
Do you ask is it upside down?
Or is it not surreal?

The colours of my palette
I mix with joy sublime
I hope one day you'll like it
And buy it for your own

We drank a gin and tonic
To ask ourselves again
Should all Art forms be understood?
Or left for Art alone?

My friend had all the answers,
If it's Art, so should it be
There is no simple problem
Someone else can never see!

BUILT TO LAST

Brick by brick, stone on stone
Mortar smoothed between
A house above a waterway
That throbs with life
In morning's light
So quiet and so serene

I've passed this way
A thousand times
But now I pause to stare
To marvel at the industry
Which brought about such symmetry
All beauty here before

I linger, then I must move on
A chill wind o'er the water
People pass by unconcerned
Yet the scene impresses as you go
For this encounter with the past
Shows how our city is built to last.

PARALLEL LINES

Run, run and run along
Never yet to meet
Each train is fleet, it's tracks unseen
Until I find this vantage point
A bridge on which to lean

Laying railways, movement swift
Do we ever pause?
All I can do is thank the guard
Who helps me with my case
A kind lady serves me tea
Dispatch official recommends
It's platform 2 he says to me.

Now I'm home, chance to reflect
A heritage of iron and steel
Takes me where I need to go
For every tunnel dug by hand
Is a testament to the power of mortal man.

RIPPLE EFFECTS

Light flickers on the water
Reflected over stone
A parapet, a tunnel effect
A wall where pigeons roost
As if to find some warmth
From cuddling up to stone.

Shelter from the icy blast
Under these iconic bridges
But I am glad to see the sun
While I walk at water's edges.

Ripples all around us
Effects for us to gauge
I feel such inspiration
A thousand memories

We never are an island
Those birds feed from our hands
Our influence is lasting
Timeless the work of our minds.

THROUGH A KEYHOLE

Stone erupted beneath the hills
A soft, honey-golden, carveable creation
Now formed as links, a parapet
Through which a structure is revealed

My modern tablet takes this shot
A pine as old as Nature's craft
Some lilies of the field exposed
Advantage taken of mortar's hold

Emerging to the sun and air
This bridge a tripod steady there
But here's a blend of engineering
Walls, lines, gravel, now a cutting
Then moving through a grassy park
Canal side boaters disembark

We lose all care, embracing now
No why or wherefore? Merely how?
A challenge to our modern lives
To take it slow, to breathe, to thrive.

SUSPENSION

The spider pauses then
Spinning resumes
A web as finest lace

As storms beat down
And dew drops cluster
He leaves his deadly trace

No mercy shown
The hapless meal, who
Flies, is trapped, then dies

But while I wait
Pondering an insect's fate
I am moved by Spider's trait

Suspended by the thinnest thread
His patient persistence
Seemingly pointless existence
Defies a wiser head.

THE DOG DAISIES

With golden heart
Such petals milky white
The green, long stem
Wild amongst buttercups
Of yellow delight

Beneath my window pane
As sun gives way to rain
While breezes brightly blow
The clover also shows

A meadow meets a forest
While here the tree is king
But on the carpeted floor
Dog daisies dance and sing

Wild roses line the hedgerows
The summer starts to fade
Flowers bloom, replaced by berries
Nuts cluster in the shade

Oh Love beguile an hour
To gather autumn fruits
For life is merely fleeting
Joy over far too soon.

LAKES OF BLUE

Swimming lakes of blue your eyes
Redolent of summer skies
Scorching, searing, then ice blue
Chilled, yet kindly, really you

In a moment I would be
Torn forever, gone from here
Yet the memory lingers on
I will therefore write this song

Singing, trilling, warbling thus
As I travel without fuss
Journeying through life's adventure
Thinking first before I mention

That I cannot give a gift
Preparing me for this, our rift
So I penned this dainty ditty
Hoping you would find it witty

On my way I quickly go
Speeding outwards, never slow
When at last I'm far from here
I will wave and wish you cheer.

THE WASHING UP

Painting the Forth Bridge
Is a thankless task
That starts the moment it ends
The washing up,
Of a sink full of mess,
Is driving me round the bend.

It only takes a few short hours
To clean the cups and the plates
But the moment it's done
There's more in the queue
The water needs changing
The 'phone starts ringing, and
I need a trip to the loo!

If I had a maid
My dishes to wash
I'd have not a trouble or care
I'd swan around town
With never a frown
And buy something new to wear!

THE NIGHT SKY

I pause and gaze upon my prey
My talons gleam in moonbeams ray
Full for harvest, the stars
Are shining, lighting the mouse
I fly at last with one swift pounce

I have the tender, little feast
No tears I cry for this poor beast
My wife expects a brood in spring
She needs her meat, and now I sing
Tu whit tu woo she hears my call
We meet to eat on farmer's wall
He's pleased to keep the vermin down
And in return he shelters us in barn
Beneath the eaves we'll build our nest
But just for now my wife rests
Her head against my breast

The morning comes, the leaves are gold
They say the owl is very old
I've hunted here as my forebears told
Now comes the sleep
For which I've yearned.

EFFORTLESS

I've heard it said
That ages gone
A squirrel could travel
From Cardiff to Merthyr
Without touching the ground
I watched in wonder
As a squirrel fled
To the highest point
Of a very high fence
Intelligent, the little beast
Scampered along the ground
Reaching, finding a suitable point
Where no barbed wire was to be found
The ease with which my furry friend
Travelled
Suggested a practice
Learnt from eons of time
Foraging for food
The squirrel was gone
Out of sight, always in mind.

I AM

I feel I am in subtle state of flux
The gamut of emotions come and go
The past is here and often haunts me much
The process of renewal seems so slow

I long for worlds another time away
For friends I've lost and scenes that are now gone
My daily task at work, at rest, at play
Is focus on the here and then move on

Advice is fast and fierce from all around
'Do this', 'do that', and never lose the fight
Each friend gives out support so very sound
I take it in and learn with all my might

But when the day is over then I rest
Review events and plan the week ahead
For when I die they'll say I did my best
And who can ask for more when they are dead.

PULTENEY WEIR

Living water, curling, cascading
Layer on layer of bubbly froth
Tumbling river overflowing
Dancing sunbeams light up Bath

See at autumn floods are flowing
Bursting banks and shrubs submerged
Flotsam, jetsam, pushing, squeezing
Over edge of water's wrath

Winter and the ice is forming
Frozen solid at the lock
Fences guard us, signposts warn us
Danger lurks on bank side path

Spring and swans are courting, nesting
Seagulls swoop and ducklings quack
Flowers bloom where once was wastage
Daffs appear and blossoms froth

At the river comes the summer
Picnics flourish, boats are back
Day trips thrive and tourists linger
Breeze is cool, we nothing lack.

STREET ART

Street Art, Graffiti
The law may be an ass
But all along our byways
Doodles invade our space
Here next ancient buildings
Of trade or corporation
Several floors of concrete
Soar above their decoration

Some Art has reached the high life
While tourists stop to gaze
Admiring the cheek of it
Disrespectful the extent of it
Who considers rights or wrongs of it?
We shrug our shoulders
Then it comes back

Along the rail embankment
Or even river bank
An all pervasive nuisance
But should you call it Art?

Whatever we determine
It will not go away
A tattoo on the city
Symbol of society's disarray.

TRIG POINT CHARLIE

I would paint this view
If painting was my skill
I would put in words
The splendour and the thrill
Of living as I do
Upon this lonely hill

I would keep in mind
The words that people say
Storing up their wisdom
To use another day

I would write a song
To chorus every dawn
And cheer my lonely night
When all else seems forlorn

When I spoke I saw
Your glorious, shining face
The sun that beams the more
Forever in this place

It was early spring
The day you came to call
Now I'm ever free
No longer just a wall.

FOR THE POLYANTHUS

Such little, dainty flowers
Appearing 'fore the spring
Cheering these cold and frosty days
With colours yellow, red and pink

Surviving cold to give us
A spot of greenery
A trace of blue or purple frill
With doubled finery

The flower that holds two colours
An amazing sight to see
How ever does it do that?
A timeless mystery

The pretty polyanthus
Like primrose in the spring
Has kept my garden lovely
Feeding the wild flown things.

THIS BITTER CHILL

Although the wind has tempered now
A deathly cold pervades this room
As if the very dead were here
I'm wrapped up like an Eskimo
Losing cheer, freezing below

Outside the spring has past its best
But way too soon to shed my vest
There is no sunshine from the West
Just cold, with icy breezes
Oh sweet summer sun, where are you now?
I seek you over hill and brow
Under earth I long to burrow
Craving warmth to soothe my sorrow
Merciless the wind and weather
I put my coat on in a lather
Several layers each on top
Of all the others, one on another
Oh sunshine sweet return to me
See me sit beneath a tree.

CRINOLINE LADY

What secrets hide behind that sweet, severe face?
Who are you? What's your story?
Such regal grace, with elegance
A moment frozen, a loved resemblance

The artist captured, set in fine china
Your image for all time now
But where have you gone?
Wistful crinoline maid
A rose in one hand held
I wonder what was the occasion?
You will never tell your tale
One can only guess your story
The finery with which you dress
Adds to the sense of mystery.
So here's a toast to miss
Unnamed, unknown but lovely
Pretty, silent, close and still,
A birthday, anniversary, festive treat
You keep it close, oh lady sweet
For I am most intrigued!
I must invent your glory!

GOODBYE SWEET FRIEND
(An Ode to Depression)

It's time to say goodbye my dear old friend
I thought this weary road would never end
But now I've reached a happier place you'll find
You're gone forever, out of sight and mind

It is such bliss to leave behind such fog
A dread companion, nemesis, black dog
You haunted me both night and day for years
I leave you now and wipe away my tears

Depression you're a dark and fearsome beast
I shrug you off, won't miss you in the least
The sun shines even on a rainy day
The work is over, now I can but play

Should you attempt to lay me waste once more
I'll take your hand and show you to my door
You are not welcome here and furthermore
I'll see you dead and live to ninety-four.

TELL ME
(For Scheherazade)

Tell me a story
Beguile my wakeful hours
Enchant the night
With songs of love
Brave deeds, or empathy
Bewitch the witching hour
Spin a yarn or two
Cloak the dark to hide it's head
Behind a screen of brighter hue
Cheering cold 'til skies are blue
Move me, please me, enrich my soul
Inspire us, educating too
For when the dawn is near us now
The day will honour you
I heard and always prove that
Your life is no longer forfeit.

ON BYRON'S BIRTHDAY

Hard frost layers the rooves
Yet warm sun roasts my face
Radio speaks of Donne, Byron, Raleigh
But the poem of Edwin Muir
Has such unexpected feeling and grace

Steam rises from neighbours boilers
Children all stay indoors
A sharp change from yesterday's rains
Sky electric blue with only one
Line of fire from a lone aeroplane

And only the blackbird sings
Silence temporarily reigns
Trees completely still, with a loud
Ticking of my clock of course, also
The pounding of my heart.

EVERYONE KNOWS SOMEONE

It's my darkest hour, no friend I find
My house is lost, my eyes are blind
I roam the streets both day and night
There's not a soul to ease my plight
The war has torn my country through
My family crossed the oceans blue
I'm left behind and never see
The value of what's meant for me
But in my pain there comes a light
A helping hand is stretched outright
Warm clothes, hot food, a mug of tea
A chance to start again, to heal
For even in my darkest day
The Lord is come and nothing grey
Shall weary all my days again
I've shelter from the sun and rain.

I AM REGIME

I am Regime
I herd your waking hours
Control the time you sleep
Despise those I call weak
The vulnerable go to the wall

I am Regime
Like clockwork am I heeded
Go elsewhere if needed
Call me cruel, I won't mind
You have no voice and
I am unkind

I am Regime
It's baked beans every Monday
Green beans every Wednesday
Endless dull repetition
No variety allowed

I am Regime
As tyrannical as Baal
The altar of my sacrifice
The clock upon the wall
Will stop one day, and all
Shall cease for we are merely temporal.

PARKING FOR PEDESTRIANS

Sitting here alone at dusk
I thought on times gone by
Reflecting while the light did fade
Sweet moments, poignant memories
A life without a care
Until you said goodbye.

You gave me all your expertise
Your love, though lost, was true
And at the dawn of era new
My heart resides with you

For now the sun sets on my dreams
But rises in the morn
Your life lives on through all our plans
And at this seat I'm joined by friends anew.

Rejoice that change will not disturb
Our voyage around the sun
And I will see you once again
When earthly days are done.

A WILTSHIRE WARRIOR

Roaming my chalk downs home
I built a hut of mud
Thatched with finest reeds
A hole for smoke to escape
Comforts for my lady
The lovely Belvedere

Wistful, wild as the briar rose
She could not be tamed
I wooed, I won, but every time
My lust she did evade

Blonde as the flax, eyes of blue
She roamed the downs by day
At night she slept beneath the moon
All hope was now removed

I joined the wars, I signed to fight
I marked my X to leave
An arrow caught my brawny chest
With Belvedere who seldom wept
I breathed, I sighed my last

She buried me with tribal style
For centuries I slept

As my dear love kept vigil guard
And mourned so many nights

Then men came with their hammers
To understand my tale
But still it's wrapped in mystery
They found her lying next to me
Her bones bleached, her broach clasped
Her arms entwined with mine.

FEAST OF GOLD
(For Ron, muse, mentor and friend for 25 years.)

Flowers delight on each occasion
Colours bright, some scents from Heaven
Here for you is this bouquet
Golden as the morning's ray
Flaming as the setting sun
When our earthly race is run.
Please accept my earnest pledge
Yellow roses, sunflowers, touch
Tinged with hints of glorious green
Colour of true love unseen.

You are mine 'til end of time
Nothing can compare to you
See the glow of golden song
Bursting forth now we are one
Everybody needs to know
I will never let you go
Pass my window, pause to pray
Just look up and there today
Is a bunch of golden scents
Come inside for redolence
You are warmly welcomed here
This a beacon, light of cheer
Every neighbour passing by

Will see that we are you and I
Me and you for evermore
Come on in, just close the door.

PERIWINKLE PICTURE

A pretty periwinkle
Flowering in February
Close to the ground
With variegated leaves
Pointed, purple or is it blue?

Here's a mindful thing to do!
Pause, stop, admire, snap
Now I've cropped it
Fixed the lighting
Here's my result
I hope you like it

Signs of spring appear today
Catkins, crocii, snowdrops too
Bulbs show promise now and later
Perfect order every year
As they appear such joy created
Helped along by gardeners too!

TURNING POINT

Here marks the spot
Of where I leave you now
We part at this our junction
To go beyond alone

It's ages since we came here
It's all so long ago
But after this our parting
I want to let you know

You'll never be forgotten
I'll keep your love in mind
And should you ever need me
My shadow walks behind

We'll be together always
Though in a different light
Alone is never lonely
When memory dogs my life

So now that it's goodbye dear
I'll raise a glass to you
We'll feast at least in spirit
With joy that's never through.

PEACE INSIDE MY HEAD

Finding words is never easy
To describe unfailing pain
Calm descends like gentle rain

Like a worry never stilled
Always anxious, won't be chilled
Leave me now as forward build

Gone the grimace, endless smile
Hiding all the angst the while
Fear behind me, peace in front

After all the years of torment
Like a child, in silence wept
Now I'm happy, tears are spent

Gone the need for reassurance
Over, all the quest for strength
Strong in this new journey's length

Join me as I travel further
Friend or sister, brother too
Let me find a home with you.

MY LIFE BY SAM THE GINGER NUT

I find it a source of much regret
That I'm the unloved Ginger Nut
Scorned by most, but loved by some
It's tough being eaten, cos then you're done

I'm fashioned in a fiery oven
Packed in plastic by the dozen
And when at last the fresh air comes
Suspended am I between your jaws

Oh I am Sam the Ginger Nut!
I'm touched with lemon, just a hint
You love me less than custard creams
But being eaten is no dream

So dunk me, dip me in your tea
I'll wallow as you swallow
It's all the same to me
For if I was as popular
As other treats - I'd feed you far
Beyond the call of duty
A Ginger Nut is Monday's booty.

THE RISE AND FALL OF TECHNOLOGY

We meet, we eat, he brings his phone
I hope it never rings
My heart is sore, my love it grieves
It is the first of many times
But with me is he there for me?
Or does he love distractions too?
A queue of bosses to talk to you
I wait in line, what do I do?

Oh chuck the wretched phone away
Put down your gadget, run and play
Laugh daily through a sunny meadow
Fling that evil in the hedgerow

Stern daughter of the voice of God
She calls him by the phone
If it was me I'd bin the thing
I'd walk it off and then I'd sing
My life is now my own.

INDEX OF FIRST LINES

A pretty periwinkle.	Page 54
A walk in autumn's golden glow.	Page 13
A window on the world.	7
Although the wind has tempered now.	40
As dusk descends with gathering gloom.	11
Brick by brick, stone on stone.	17
Bright, blazing, beautiful, blue sky.	9
Colder, darker, lagging dawn.	3
Drizzle damping silent falls.	12
Finding words is never easy.	58
Flowers delight on each occasion.	52
Hard frost layers the rooves.	46
Here marks the spot.	56
I am Regime.	48
I feel I am in subtle state of flux.	33
I find it a source of much regret.	59
I gaze with deepest love.	15
I pause and gaze upon my prey.	30
I would paint this view.	37
I've heard it said.	31
It's my darkest hour, no friend I find.	47

It's time to say goodbye my dear, old friend.	43
Light flickers on the water.	21
Like a glorious, tumbling waterfall.	16
Living water, curling, cascading.	35
Painting the Forth Bridge.	29
Roaming my chalk downs home.	51
Run, run and run along.	19
Sitting here alone at dusk.	49
Stone erupted beneath the hills.	23
Storm Arwen blew its' way.	1
Street Art, Graffiti.	36
Such little, dainty flowers.	39
Sunshine, yellow roses.	5
Swimming lakes of blue your eyes.	28
Tell me a story.	45
The spider pauses then.	25
What secrets hide behind that sweet, severe face?	41
With golden heart.	27

ACKNOWLEDGMENTS

I would like to thank Sally Collister for able assistance and mentoring of my photography in its early days. I would also like to thank Bath MIND for all their support and for providing a brilliant atmosphere for the photography group in and around Bath, England.

Thanks are also due to HM government's Department for Work and Pensions for providing the funding for this publication.

www.ingramcontent.com/pod-product-compliance
Lightning Source LLC
Chambersburg PA
CBHW070336120526
44590CB00017B/2901